Free DV)

Essential Test Tips DVD from Trivium Test Prep

Dear Customer,

Thank you for purchasing from Cirrus Test Prep! Whether you're looking to join the military, get into college, or advance your career, we're honored to be a part of your journey.

To show our appreciation (and to help you relieve a little of that test-prep stress), we're offering a **FREE *Praxis Essential Test Tips DVD*** by Cirrus Test Prep. Our DVD includes 35 test preparation strategies that will help keep you calm and collected before and during your big exam. All we ask is that you email us your feedback and describe your experience with our product. Amazing, awful, or just so-so: we want to hear what you have to say!

To receive your **FREE *Praxis Essential Test Tips DVD***, please email us at 5star@cirrustestprep.com. Include "Free 5 Star" in the subject line and the following information in your email:

1. The title of the product you purchased.
2. Your rating from 1 – 5 (with 5 being the best).
3. Your feedback about the product, including how our materials helped you meet your goals and ways in which we can improve our products.
4. Your full name and shipping address so we can send your **FREE *Praxis Essential Test Tips DVD***.

If you have any questions or concerns please feel free to contact us directly at 5star@cirrustestprep.com. Thank you, and good luck with your studies!

* Please note that the free DVD is <u>not included</u> with this book. To receive the free DVD, please follow the instructions above.

Praxis II Principles of Learning and Teaching Early Childhood Rapid Review Flash Cards

Exam Prep Including 250+ Flash Cards for the Praxis PLT 5621 Test

Introduction

Congratulations on choosing to take the Praxis II Principles of Learning and Teaching: Early Childhood (5621) exam! By purchasing this book, you've taken the first step toward becoming an educator.

This guide will provide you with a detailed overview of the Praxis II PLT: Early Childhood (5621) exam, so you know exactly what to expect on test day. We'll take you through all the concepts covered on the test and give you the opportunity to test your knowledge with practice questions. Even if it's been a while since you last took a major test, don't worry; we'll make sure you're more than ready!

What is the Praxis?

Praxis tests are a part of teaching licensure in approximately forty states. Each state uses the tests and scores in different ways, so be sure to check the certification requirements in your state by going to www.ets.org/praxis/states. There, you will find information detailing the role of the Praxis tests in determining teaching certification in your state, what scores are required, and how to transfer Praxis scores from one state to another.

What's on the Praxis?

The content in this guide will prepare you for the Praxis II Principles of Learning and Teaching: Early Childhood (5621) exam. This test assesses whether you possess the knowledge and skills necessary to become a teacher, using both multiple-choice questions and writing assignments. The test always has a total of seventy multiple-choice questions and four constructed-response questions; however the number of questions specific to each content category is approximate (see the following table). The constructed-response questions are based on two case histories describing classroom or professional scenarios. Each case is followed by two prompts. Your responses should analyze the scenarios and demonstrate your understanding of the principles of teaching.

You have a maximum of two hours to complete the entire test. We recommend that you spend approximately fifty minutes on the constructed-response questions and seventy minutes on the multiple-choice questions, but you may use the two hours allotted as you see fit.

Praxis II Principles of Learning and Teaching: Early Childhood (5621) Content		
Concepts	**Approximate Number of Questions**	**Percentage**
Students as Learners	21 multiple-choice	22.5%
Instructional Process	21 multiple-choice	22.5%
Assessment	14 multiple-choice	15%
Professional Development, Leadership, and Community	14 multiple-choice	15%
Analysis of Instructional Scenarios	4 constructed-response	
Students as Learners	1 – 2 questions	
Instructional Process	1 – 2 questions	25%
Assessment	0 – 1 questions	
Professional Development, Leadership, and Community	0 – 1 questions	
Total (2 hours)	70 multiple-choice 4 constructed-response	

You will answer approximately twenty-one multiple-choice and one or two constructed-response questions on Students as Learners. You should have a solid understanding of human developmental processes, student diversity, and learning goals and objectives. This section will assess your aptitude for managing the behavior of students and creating a productive and organized learning atmosphere. As a teacher, your classroom should feel safe for your students and be conducive to excellence, equity, and learning.

You will answer approximately twenty-one multiple-choice and one or two constructed-response questions on Instructional Process. Planning instruction is important for engaging and motivating students. You should be able to use communication methods, instructional strategies, and questioning techniques to deliver instruction in different contexts.

You will be given approximately fourteen multiple-choice and possibly one constructed-response question on Assessment. Your teaching should incorporate assessment that monitors student achievement, understanding, and performance, and feedback that is helpful, flexible, and timely. Testing tools and how they can be used to assess students will be covered in this section.

You will answer approximately fourteen multiple-choice and possibly one constructed-response question on Professional Development, Leadership, and Community. Your role as a teacher will include serving as an advocate and resource for learners, their families, and administration; you should be able to communicate effectively with families and other professionals. This section will assess your knowledge of an educator's ethical and legal requirements as well as the resources available to help you as a teacher in the education system.

How is the Praxis Scored?

The preceding table offers a breakdown of the concepts covered on the Praxis. Your score report will also show a breakdown of the raw points scored in each content category. The seventy multiple-choice questions are equally weighted and account for 75 percent of your overall score. Keep in mind that some multiple-choice questions are experimental questions for the purpose of the Praxis test writers and will not count toward your overall score. However, since those questions are not indicated on the test, you must respond to every question. There is no penalty for guessing on Praxis tests, so be sure to eliminate incorrect answer choices and answer every question. If you still do not know the answer, guess; you may get it right!

On the constructed-response section, the graders of the responses assign a score of 0 – 2 to each response. A score of a 2 is earned by a response that shows a thorough understanding of the prompt by being accurate and complete, while a score of a 1 will be given to an answer that shows a basic understanding of the prompt with a mostly weak or incomplete answer. A response that does not answer the questions or that demonstrates misunderstanding will receive a score of 0. The scores of the four constructed-response essays are equally weighted to comprise 25 percent of your overall score.

Your score report will be available two to three weeks after the test date and will stay on your Praxis account for one year, but you can also opt for a paper report. The score report includes your score and the passing score for the states you identified as score recipients.

How is the Praxis Administered?

The Praxis tests are available at testing centers across the nation. To find a testing center near you, go to http://www.ets.org/praxis/register. At this site, you can create a Praxis account, check testing dates, register for a test, or find instructions for registering via mail or phone. The Praxis II Principles of Learning and Teaching: Early Childhood (5621) exam is administered as a computerized test. The Praxis website allows you to take a practice test to acclimate yourself to the computerized format.

On the day of your test, be sure to bring your admission ticket (which is provided when you register) and photo ID. The testing facility will provide an area outside of the testing room to store your personal belongings. You are allowed no personal effects in the testing area. Cell phones and other electronic, photographic, recording, or listening devices are not permitted in the testing center at all, and bringing those items may be cause for dismissal, forfeiture of your testing fees, and cancellation of your scores. For details on what is and is not permitted at your testing center, refer to http://www. ets.org/praxis/test_day/bring.

About Cirrus Test Prep

Cirrus Test Prep study guides are designed by current and former educators and are tailored to meet your needs as an incoming educator. Our guides offer all of the resources necessary to help you pass teacher certification tests across the nation.

Cirrus clouds are graceful, wispy clouds characterized by their high altitude. Just like cirrus clouds, Cirrus Test Prep's goal is to help educators "aim high" when it comes to obtaining their teacher certification and entering the classroom.

About This Guide

This guide will help you master the most important test topics and also develop critical test-taking skills. We have built features into our books to prepare you for your tests and increase your score. Along with a detailed summary of the test's format, content, and scoring, we offer an in-depth overview of the content knowledge required to pass the test. Our sidebars provide interesting information, highlight key concepts, and review content so that you can solidify your understanding of the exam's concepts. Test your knowledge with sample questions and detailed answer explanations in the text that help you think through exam problems, as well as with practice tests that reflect the content and format of the Praxis. We're pleased you've chosen Cirrus to be a part of your professional journey.

guided practice

John Dewey

direct teaching

practicing a new concept with scaffolded support from the teacher

a pragmatic philosopher who viewed learning as a series of scientific inquiry and experimentation; he advocated real-world experiences and volunteerism

a form of teaching that is centered on the teacher and instruction is based on disseminating facts

recall

operant conditioning

short-term memory

the act of retrieving facts

provides rewards or punishment as a motivation for desired performance

information that enters the conscious memory but is not stored for recall at a later time

motor disabilities

reciprocal determinism

standard deviation

characterized by loss of movement; may be caused by injury or disease

the theory by Albert Bandura which states that behavior is determined by a combination of cognitive factors, the environment, and stimuli

a mathematical calculation that indicates the variability of scores in comparison with the average

one-on-one

Abraham Maslow

reading guides

a type of instruction in which a teacher works with one individual student on a concept

developed the hierarchy of needs, which he theorized to be the unconscious desires that motivate people

guides that include statements or questions that lead students through the text, providing instructional focus

median

distance learning

verbal prompting

the middle score if all scores were lined up from least to greatest

a type of learning that involves provisions for educating students that are not in attendance at a school facility

using words or beginning phonemes to assist students

inductive reasoning

schema

restatement

conclusions are drawn by putting together known concepts and applying them to a new situation

the framework of understanding in a child's brain

when the learner or listener repeats what has been learned using his or her own wording

cognitive dissonance theory

workshops

performance

uneasiness is felt when an individual has conflicting thoughts

discussions or meetings in which participants come together to interact and exchange information about best practices

when students present their learning as teachers watch to assess mastery of learning goals

conference

assertive discipline

interdisciplinary unit

a meeting between teacher and student in which learning is orally assessed and evaluated

a classroom management technique in which the teacher takes clear control over the classroom and its dynamics

a unit of study in which content from all subject areas is integrated

differentiation

self-efficacy

punishment

providing curriculum for students based on their individual needs, including learning styles and level

when a person believes that he or she is capable of achieving a learning goal

penalizing for the purpose of extinguishing behavior

computer-mediated instruction

small group

classic conditioning

learning activities facilitated through computer technology

instruction provided to a group composed of learners with similar instructional needs

learning a response to stimuli or the environment

questioning

mode

situated motivation

inquiries that are used to help focus instruction and assess understanding

the score that appears most frequently

a form of extrinsic motivation when a student is motivated, but only within the particular context of the situation

long-term memory

learning centers

coaching

information that is stored for a long period of time and may be recalled

segments of the classroom in which independent learning activities are provided to students

training that occurs when one person receives support from another toward the achievement of a goal

synthesize

convergent questions

attribution theory

the process of combining information from various sources and applying it to a new area

questions that have a clear, correct answer

internal attribution is assumed when other people make mistakes or are victims, as individuals tend to see others as a predictable stereotype; when an individual makes a mistake, he or she tends to view the cause as external

visual impairments

audio aid

physical domain

problems with eyesight, such as blindness

a device that amplifies the teacher's speech so that it can be heard clearly by students

all aspects of motor skill development; also called the psycho-motor domain

interactive learning

basic interpersonal communication
skills (BICS)

rubric

a learning approach that relies heavily on social interaction and cooperative grouping

language needed to interact in face-to-face social situations

a fixed scale that measures performance with detailed descriptions of criteria that define each level of performance

**Title IX of the Education
Amendments of 1972**

extrinsic motivation

intrinsic motivation

protects students against gender discrimination in all federally funded education programs, including colleges that receive federal funding

an external reward

an internal reward

Jerome Bruner

incident analysis

formative assessment

a constructivist theorist who contributed the three modes of representation to the field of cognitive development

a formal review of an incident to determine why it happened and how to reduce the likelihood of another similar event

informal assessments that are used throughout the learning experiences to help teachers make instructional decisions and to provide feedback to students

scope

exit ticket

stakeholder

outlines the learning objectives that will be taught to students, including all supporting standards and the level of complexity

a small piece of paper that includes two to three short, literal comprehension questions; a useful tool for teachers to assess student understanding at the end of a lesson in order to better shape future lessons

anyone who has a stake in the school; includes students, teachers, parents, staff, administrators, and community members

models

inquiry

equal access

representations or examples

the process of finding the answers to questions

provides procedural safeguards to ensure that all students receive the same benefits of public education regardless of disabilities

criterion-referenced test

English-language learners (ELL)

Lawrence Kohlberg

measure students according to performance on preset standards

students whose native language is not English

identified the stages of moral development

industry vs. inferiority

document-based question (DBQ)

licensing

a stage in Erik Erikson's theory of psychosocial development; children are in school and are exposed to new materials, new people, and new experiences; for the first time, children are compared to a standard and assessed by others

contains three to fifteen primary and secondary source documents that all relate to a single question; an important assessment tool in social studies

to be given permission to do something or to use something that belongs to someone else

nonverbal prompting

tenure

Common Core Standards

using gestures or other physical prompts to assist students

a person who has been given a permanent position; tenured teachers have earned only the right to due process

the predominant set of standards used across most states for Math and English Language Arts

standardized test

critical thinking

predict

a test administered to all students in a consistent way and then graded in the same way so that score comparisons may be accurately made

looking at evidence from an objective viewpoint to make inferences or draw conclusions

the act of anticipating what will happen

think time

First Amendment

Albert Bandura

the processing time that a learner takes after receiving new information before responding to it

guarantees freedom of religion, freedom of expression, freedom of the press, and freedom to peaceably assemble

a Canadian psychologist who developed the social learning theory

scoring guide

---

curriculum-based measures

---

validity

a guide that measures performance with detailed descriptions of criteria that define each level of performance and that are weighted with multipliers

measures that determine student progress and performance based on specific lessons presented in the unit

indicates how well an assessment measures what it is intended to measure; a test is not considered valid if it is not reliable

action plan

psychomotor objectives

knowledge

a process by which goals and the steps toward achieving those goals are determined

objectives that focus on student skills (tasks or actions they can execute)

acquired intellectual information

continuum

lecture

code-switching

a progression of learning

teacher-led instruction; the teacher talks while the students listen and possibly take notes

when students slip into native language while speaking their second-language or vice versa

constructivism

Americans with Disabilities Act

exceptionality

when students construct their own knowledge through learning experiences

prohibits discrimination based on disabilities; in schools, this includes activities that take place both on and off campus, including athletics and extracurricular activities

strength or weakness in academic functioning that requires extra attention to meet the needs of the student

role play

research projects

remediation

using playacting to demonstrate a concept

studies of specific concepts using scientific principles for gathering information

the additional support provided to regular education students to bridge gaps in learning

bias

the six levels in Benjamin Bloom's
cognitive domain

divergent questions

an unfair inclination toward a person or idea that invalidates objectivity

Level 1: Remembering
Level 2: Understanding
Level 3: Applying
Level 4: Analyzing
Level 5: Evaluating
Level 6: Creating

open-ended questions designed to assess a student's ability to analyze, evaluate, and create

liability

due process

Howard Gardner

a legal responsibility

everyone must be treated fairly, and the rights of all must be respected

created the theory of multiple intelligences; proposed that using a person's area of giftedness to demonstrate intellect will help learners achieve their potential

cognitive academic language
proficiency (CALPS)

independent learning

intellectual freedom

a student's ability to comprehend academic vocabulary in English

learning experiences that are completed autonomously by the student

the right to receive information from various perspectives without censorship

speech disorders

selected response

concept mapping

difficulty forming words

students choose the best answer from the available choices; sometimes called multiple choice

the practice of using graphic organizers to present thoughts or information

contrast

Erik Erikson

compare

when students note the differences between two or more things

his theory of psychosocial development focuses on reconciling individual needs with needs of society through stages

when students note the similarities between two or more things

portfolio

essay test

English Language Proficiency
Standards (ELPS)

a collection of a student's work as evidence of learning to be evaluated using portfolio assessments

written responses to questions that provide students the opportunity to fully articulate their learning

objectives that not only support ESL instruction, but also increase student's academic readiness in the content areas

anecdotal notes

professional associations

copyright

written records of the teacher's observations of a student; records should be specific, objective, and focused on outlined criteria

nonprofit organizations that are formed to support the members of a particular profession by setting standards and advocating for their members

the exclusive right to intellectual works, such as literary or musical pieces

simulations

learning communities

summarize

models that mimic real-world processes

small groups of professionals who share common goals that meet to collaborate about instructional practices

when an individual provides a condensed version of a story or an explanation

analytical scoring

intellectually gifted

psychosocial development theory

breaks down the general categories to be scored into more specific parts

students with an IQ greater than 130

the theory that there are eight stages in human development, with each stage centered on a different social conflict; the resolution of each conflict will either move the individual forward in development or stunt his or her growth, resulting in negative emotions and behaviors

physical disabilities

classical conditioning

cognitive objectives

impairments that require assistance during the school day

a neutral stimulus becomes associated with a reflex response through conditioning

focus on student learning

categorize

mentor

positive reinforcement

the practice of sorting into groups by characteristics

a more experienced professional who guides someone who is newer to the profession

encouraging a behavior to continue or improve by providing the student with something he or she values such as praise, recognition, or rewards

paraprofessional

---

problem-based learning

Gardner's nine intelligences

a trained teacher assistant

---

learning by solving open-ended questions

---

verbal-linguistic (language)

logical-mathematical (abstractions and patterns)

spatial-visual (thinks in pictures)

bodily-kinesthetic (movement)

musical (rhythm, pitch, and timber)

interpersonal (empathy)

intrapersonal (self-aware)

naturalist (plants, animals)

existential (deep thinker)

positive behavioral supports

diagnostic assessment

learning theories

a social learning approach that assumes all persistent behavior choices are logical, so a persistent misbehavior must serve some kind of purpose

given before a learning experience to measure the students' baseline knowledge

describe how genetics, development, environment, motivation, and emotions affect a student's ability to acquire and apply knowledge

age-equivalent score

teachable moment

grade-equivalent scores

found using the average score of students within an age group

when an unplanned event occurs, triggering interest in learning more about a related topic

found using the average score of students who fall into that grade

visual aid

vicarious learning

physical therapist

something that can be shown to students to accompany text or speech in order to clarify meaning

a theory by Albert Bandura that involves learning by observing the consequences to others that evokes emotion from the observer

a type of therapist that is a certified professional who evaluates and treats mobility issues

modeling

Section 504 of the Rehabilitation Act

---

extrinsic rewards

demonstrating for others so that they can learn through mimicry

provides services to all students in federally assisted programs who have physical or mental impairments that substantially limit one or more life activities

external rewards, such as trinkets, praise, or recognition, bestowed upon someone for doing a good job

behaviorism

raw score

reflective journal

a theory of behaviorism that describes how rewards and punishments condition student behavior and learning

the number of questions a student answered correctly

records of a learning experience

Benjamin Bloom

---

language acquisition

---

holistic scoring

contributed to the taxonomy of educational objectives and the theory of mastery learning

the process by which a new language is learned

uses general categories to rate the overall outcome

Edward Thorndike

moral domain

wait time

Thorndike's research initially led to operant conditioning; Thorndike's learning laws include the law of effect, the law of readiness, and the law of exercise

the acquisition of morals and values

processing time that is intentionally provided by the teacher after asking a question to give learners think time

social domain

intrinsic rewards

transfer

also referred to as the affective or social-emotional domain; includes emotions, motivation, and attitudes

when learners are internally satisfied by doing work because it is interesting, challenging, or relevant, or makes them feel successful

applying knowledge to make inferences about new thoughts and ideas

peer practice

percentile

self-determination theory

the practice of using social interaction among students to promote learning goals

ranks a student in comparison with what percentage of students measured higher and what percentage of students measured lower

everyone has a perceived locus of causality

vocal stress

divergent thinkers

enrichment

emphasizing a word or words to convey meaning

people who think more deeply and differently from other people

the opportunity to learn objectives at a deeper level than outlined in the curriculum standards

viewing guides

the five levels in Benjamin Bloom's affective domain

Lev Vygotsky

guides that include statements or questions that provide instructional focus while students are watching films or clips

Level 1: Awareness
Level 2: Responding
Level 3: Valuing
Level 4: Organization
Level 5: Characterization

a Russian psychologist who researched what has become the social development theory; more knowledgeable other (MKO) and zone of proximal development (ZPD) are the two main tenets of his philosophy

self-regulate

foundational theorists

deductive reasoning

to maintain control of one's own emotional responses

---

the people who provided the framework by which all current knowledge of cognitive processes is based

---

conclusions are drawn by using known information and narrowing it to a specific circumstance

think-pair-shares

cooperative learning

Jean Piaget

students reflect on a question individually and then turn to other students nearby to share and discuss their responses

the teacher places students into small groups and gives them a task to complete together

a Swiss psychologist who was the first to study cognition in children, and identified stages of development and contributed to schema learning

learning styles

concept learning

artifacts

the different ways in which children learn

form of learning that involves classifying information by topic

genuine objects or articles created by a person

manipulatives

scaffolds

mapping

items that students are able to move or change during hands-on instruction

the supports that allow a child to work above his or her independent level and are gradually removed as the learner gains mastery

the practice of graphically organizing thoughts by starting with a main idea and organizing thoughts and ideas around the main idea

Socratic Method

task analysis

confidentiality

a teaching technique in which a leader prompts discussion solely by asking questions and allowing the class to share and then respond to and build upon one another's ideas

the teacher takes a larger, complex goal and breaks it down into smaller, concrete components that lead to the ultimate goal

the ability to be trusted with private information

analyze

Piaget's Theory of Development

John Watson

the process of inspecting something critically

the theory that human development occurs in four general stages: sensorimotor, preoperational, concrete operational, and formal operational

coined the term behaviorism, which objectively measures behavior in response to stimuli

memory

cloze procedures

B.F. Skinner

a cognitive process of storing and retrieving information that has been learned

the practice of omitting words from the text as a reading comprehension activity

expanded on operant conditioning, but focused on responding to environment in lieu of responding to stimuli

peer assessment

lesson objective

debates

evaluation and feedback among students

establishes the student's learning goals for a lesson

formal discussions about opposing arguments

motivation theory

planning

assessment

explains the driving forces behind conduct

having forethought in implementation and design to achieve a desired outcome

the process of gathering data to determine the extent to which learning goals have been met

achievement test

psychomotor domain

privacy

tests that measure acquired knowledge or skills

controls motor skill development

freedom from having personal business shared with others

schemata

Next Generation Science Standards

ability test

rules by which individuals understand the world around them

science standards released in 2012 that are similar in style and purpose to the Common Core Standards

measure a person's ability to perform a particular skill

individualized education plan (IEP)

pair/share

Bloom's Taxonomy

an annual meeting for each special education student that outlines the student's learning goals and identifies the accommodations and modifications that will be offered to the student

students work with a partner to discuss learning as it is taking place

a framework for categorizing educational goals that identifies six categories based on the three domains of learning (psychomotor, affective, and cognitive)

observation

modifications

creative thinking

when a teacher watches a student engaged in a learning activity to find evidence of learning

changes made to the curriculum because students are so far behind that they are unable to use the same curriculum as their peers

describes cognitive processes, such as brainstorming, that are designed to generate new thoughts, ideas, and solutions experiential learning

Lawrence Kohlberg's six stages of
moral development

zone of proximal development (ZPD)

a type of learning that happens through experiences and may include hands-on learning

Stage 1: Obedience and Punishment Orientation

Stage 2: Individualism and Exchange

Stage 3: Good Interpersonal Relationships

Stage 4: Maintaining the Social Order

Stage 5: Social Contract and Individual Rights

Stage 6: Universal Principles

the space between what a child can do independently and the learning goal

cloze questions

---

redirect

---

reflective listening

fill-in-the-blank questions

distracting students from negative behavior by channeling their attention into something positive

when the teacher hears a speaker and then repeats back the meaning behind their words in order to clarify understanding

brainstorming

learning domain

occupational therapist

the process of generating ideas related to a specific problem or concept

the three domains of learning are cognitive, affective, and psychomotor

a certified professional who assesses and provides treatment for the development of life skills among disabled individuals

critical friend

choice theory

affective domain

someone who supports growth by providing objective and honest feedback

theory developed by William Glasser which posits that behavior is not separate from choice; behavior is divided behavior into four categories: acting, thinking, feeling, and physiology

controls the development of emotions, values, and attitudes

problem-solving

engage

achievement motivation

the process of finding answers to difficult questions

inspiring interest or motivation

the desire to continually seek greater challenges; it includes the desire to increase one's sense of competency, self-esteem, or self-actualization—all intrinsic motivators

speech therapist

---

summative assessment

SMART goals

a certified professional who diagnoses and treats communication disorders

formal or informal assessments that evaluate student achievement after learning takes place

Specific, Measurable, Achievable, Relevant, Time-bound

cognitive disabilities

indirect teaching

metacognition

impairments in intellectual functioning and adaptive behavior

student-centered instruction in which the teacher facilitates opportunities for students to construct their own learning

thinking about learning process

assimilation

reliability

infer

incorporating new learning into existing schemata

the consistency of similar results if the test were repeated; s test can be reliable even if it is not valid

drawing a conclusion using reasoning skills

accommodations

vocal tone

cognitive domain

provide access to the same curriculum as their grade-level peers, but information is presented in a different way

a certain way of sounding that expresses meaning

the ways students process new information, store knowledge, and retrieve it to apply to new circumstances

mean

whole class

instructional pacing

the average score

when instruction is delivered to all of the students in the class at the same time in the same way

how quickly a teacher moves through the content and related activities

gesture

integrative framework

explicit teaching

a movement intended to nonverbally convey meaning

a plan for achieving goals in all subject areas by combining content across disciplines

focused and unambiguous teaching of a specific skill or standard

cognitive domain

formal assessment

conferences (professional development)

acquiring intellect

assessments that measure student progress using standardized measures

formal meetings that are typically sponsored by a professional association in which members of a particular profession come together to learn from one another and discuss important topics within the field

informal assessment

norm referenced

language impairments

Informal assessments are collected in the classroom to monitor student performance

tests that measure students in comparison with other students of the same age

difficulty with comprehension

standards-based education

demonstrations

skills

education based on a set of learning outcomes clearly set by the district and state that all students are expected to achieve

the practice of providing evidence of an observable conclusion

ability to apply what has been learned

thematic unit

affective objectives

cognitive processes

integrating curricula across content areas under a general theme

focus on student feelings and values

acquiring new knowledge and skills and being able to apply new learning to new situations and draw conclusions from it

identity vs. role confusion

reinforcement

evaluate

a stage in Erik Erikson's theory of psychosocial development; individuals aged 12 – 18 try out different friends, styles, and belief systems on their way to figuring out why they are

the process of strengthening behavior through rewards or consequences

when something or someone is assessed

learning contracts

self-assessment

discovery learning

agreements negotiated between a student and a teacher, with possible input from other school personnel or parents, designed for the improvement of an objective

a method by which students monitor their own progress toward learning goals

when students perform experiments or research information to comprehend new concepts

classroom management

internships

analytical checklist

active management of the physical classroom space, the culture of the classroom, and individual student behavior

positions that offer on-the-job training either in addition to or in lieu of a salary

outlines of criteria of student performance that teachers check off as students show mastery of each required skill

aptitude test

active listening

vocal inflection

measure a person's ability to develop a particular skill

improves listening skills by structuring how a person listens and responds to the person who is talking

a change of pitch or tone to express meaning

sequence

self-motivation

feedback

the order in which learning objectives are taught to maximize student success

the drive from within that inspires a person to work toward something

information about performance

generalize

listening guides

**Individuals with Disabilities
Education Act (IDEA)**

the practice of applying what is known from a small sample and assuming it to be true about a larger group

statements or questions that provide instructional focus when listening to a lecture or other form of auditory instruction

provides guidelines to schools to help address the individual needs of special education students

knowledge

symbolic stage

enactive state

acquired information

stage during which children aged 1 – 6 learn through abstractions such as language, symbols, and classifications; proposed by Jerome Bruner

stage during which children aged 0 – 1 year learn through action; proposed by Jerome Bruner

Albert Bandura's four processes for
behavior change

Family Educational Rights and Privacy
Act of 1974

authentic language

attention, retention, reproduction, and motivation

prohibits schools from sharing identifiable information about students

reading materials from books, newspapers, the Internet and other real-life sources

self-actualization

lesson planning

the final state in Maslow's hierarchy of needs; the individual has realized their potential and seeks fulfillment and growth

the alignment of standards, assessments, and learning materials to create a learning trajectory for a course of instruction